Stations of the Resurrection

JESUS

Raymond Chapman is Emeritus Professor of English Literature at the University of London and a non-stipendiary priest in the Diocese of Southwark. He is a Vice-Chairman of the Prayer Book Society and is the author of numerous literary and religious books including *Rhythms of Prayer* and *Stations of the Nativity*, both to be published in 1999 by Morehouse Publishing.

STATIONS
of the
Resurrection

*Meditations on the Fourteen
Resurrection Appearances*

Raymond Chapman

MOREHOUSE PUBLISHING

Copyright © 1998 by Raymond Chapman

Illustrations © see pp. 61–66

Originally published in English under the title *Stations of the Resurrection* by the Canterbury Press Norwich, St. Mary's Works, St. Mary's Plain, Norwich, Norfolk NR3 3BH UK

Morehouse Publishing
P.O. Box 1321
Harrisburg, PA 17105

Morehouse Publishing is a division of The Morehouse Group.

Printed in the United States of America

Cover design by Corey Kent

Library of Congress Cataloging-in-Publication Data

Chapman, Raymond.
    Stations of the Resurrection : meditations on the fourteen Resurrection appearances / Raymond Chapman.
        p.   cm.
    Includes bibliographical references.
    ISBN 0-8192-1788-3 (pbk.)
    1. Jesus Christ—Appearances—Prayer-books and devotions—English. I. Title.
BT490.C48 1999
232.9′7—dc21   98-49528
                                                    CIP

Contents

Suggestions for Using this Book

The Way of the Cross is a traditional exercise of devotion, in which we follow with awe and penitence the steps of Jesus to Calvary and the tomb. Even in their sorrow, Christians know that the glorious Resurrection completes the story and brings the power of the Risen Christ into the world until the end of time. Here we may contemplate the Resurrection experiences of the disciples and join with them in joy and praise for victory over death.

The Resurrection appearances are here set out in fourteen stations. The meditations and prayers accompanying each of them may be used for either personal or corporate devotion, as the Stations of the Cross are used by many worshippers. In a conducted progress around a church, in gathered prayer or in private reflection, the devotion may be particularly suitable for the forty days of the Easter season, but also for any time in the year except perhaps in Lent, for the power of the

Resurrection is always present.

Each of the stations has the relevant biblical passage, a short consideration and prayers of thanksgiving and penitence with versicles and responses to introduce and link each station. Pictures are added which may aid devotion. Suggested prayers and hymns for beginning and ending the whole devotion may be appropriate when it is led by a conductor.

All the stations here set out are based on biblical witness. It is not necessary to try to harmonize them into a continuous narrative; each reveals some truth of the experience of the witnesses, and of ourselves.

For more extended use of the stations, each has a longer meditation focusing more fully on what that particular appearance of our Lord may be saying to us and more intimately relating it to the witness or witnesses. These meditations are probably most suitable for individual devotion with one or a few stations at a time. It is suggested that those following this method read more fully in the biblical account where it is appropriate; some, like the appearance to James, have only short references. You may wish to pass first through the shorter devotions of the station as a preparation for meditation and resolution.

Introduction

The Resurrection of Jesus Christ is central to our Christian faith and has been so from the beginning. It is the proof and promise that he was not just an inspired human teacher or a righteous man, but the incarnate Son of God, who lived a fully human life even to death, but overcame death and was raised to glory. Our Christian Sunday celebrates the day of Resurrection on the first day of the week as told in the Gospels.

The biblical witnesses record several experiences of the presence of Christ in the forty days between the Resurrection and the Ascension. They tell of their meetings with one who was identical with the Teacher they had loved and followed, yet wonderfully transformed. The change of mood in the disciples after the desolation of Good Friday, the new confidence and firmness of purpose with which they went out to preach the good news and begin the work of the Church, are the strongest testimony to the reality of their experiences.

Almost every book of the New Testament directly refers to the Resurrection; all are founded on the faith of Christ raised from the dead. It was a mighty act of God, not a solution to a sudden disaster, but ordained for the completion of the Incarnation and the salvation of the world.

The evidences about the risen Body agree in several ways. This was not resuscitation of one apparently dead, or the resumption of former life as had occurred at the raising of Lazarus, the daughter of Jairus and the widow's son at Nain. The body in which the Risen Christ appeared was free of time and space, not restricted by such human barriers as closed doors. Yet this was not a ghost or disembodied spirit, for the new body was palpable to touch and could join his friends at meals as in the past. The witnesses had no doubt that this glorified Lord was the same as the Jesus who had called them to follow him.

The bodily Resurrection of Christ on earth lasted for forty days. It culminated in the Ascension, which was not the withdrawal of his power and love from us, but the beginning of a new dispensation. It ensures that the human race participates in his glory, because it was his humanity as well as his divinity that has entered into heaven. Thus heaven is not just a remote spiritual realm detached from this world, but a reality for the perpetual healing and strengthening of those who still walk on earth as Christ walked before.

Christians live in the Easter faith because we have not only the past witness but the abiding presence of Christ with the faithful. When St Paul writes of 'Christ in me' he is not using just a figure of speech. Christ was raised from the dead for our justification (Rom. 4:25); the Atonement brought by his Passion is made effective in all who believe that he lives for us as he died for us. We share in the totality of sacrificial love through suffering to glory. This is represented and received in our baptism when we symbolically die with him and are raised with him (Col. 2:12).

The Resurrection of Christ is our present strength and our future hope. It is the guarantee of our own resurrection, clearly promised and affirmed in scripture and creeds. We are already sharers in his life (Col. 3:1–4; Eph. 2:5–6). Humanity is given the double victory of redemption from sin and triumph over death until the end of time when God's purpose is completed (1 Cor. 15:20–24).

We can discern signs of resurrection all around us in this world. We are reminded of it in the year-ly renewal of nature; in recovery from illness; in forgiveness and reconciliation after estrangement; in all new hopes and fresh starts. All these mani-fest the restoring power of God's love, but are only types of the great mystery that lies beneath them.

We should cultivate a greater theology of joy. It is right that Christians, individually and collectively, should care much for the great troubles of the world and try to join them with the suffering of Christ, committing to his love the many things that we cannot explain or understand. But perhaps we have given too little attention to the goodness and happiness of human life, the many good gifts of God. Concentration on the Cross will strengthen our endurance and our compassion for others. Meditation on the Resurrection will help us to make occasions of thankfulness enter more deeply into our devotions.

Yet penitence can never be far away; as we become more aware of the goodness of God, we become more aware also of our own sinfulness and ingratitude. That is why in each of these stations an offering of thanks is followed by an acknowledgement of sin and a prayer for help to do better. We need to give our limited minds to one consideration at a time but our relationship with God is not contained in closed compartments. All prayer – adoration, thanksgiving, penitence, petition and intercession – is gathered in the Resurrection faith: 'Christ is risen: he is risen indeed.'

Before the Stations

Almighty God, whose blessed Son appeared in his Risen Body to many who believed in him, give us grace so to meditate on the mystery of his Resurrection that we may see him with the eyes of faith, and be united with him in eternal life, where he reigns in the unity of the Blessed Trinity, Father, Son and Holy Spirit, ever one God, world without end. Amen.

A hymn may be sung; the following are suitable:

'Christ the Lord is risen again'

'Come, let us join our cheerful songs'

'Lord enthroned in heavenly splendour'

'Love's redeeming work is done'

1

Earthquake

V   We adore thee O Christ and we bless thee.
R   **Because by thy glorious Resurrection thou hast
given life to the world.**

*Suddenly there was a great earthquake; for an
angel of the Lord, descending from heaven, came
and rolled back the stone and sat on it.* (Matt. 28:2)

They had sealed the stone and set a watch, thinking that they had seen the last of Jesus. God broke
through their strongest guard with the power of
his love. Nothing could hold back the new life that
had come into the world to overcome death for
ever.

We give thanks for the power that is infinite yet
comes so gently to meet all our needs; for every
showing of that power in the natural world and in
human lives; for the way in which people can be
changed by a single touch of the love of God.

   We think that our problems are too great, our
sins too bad for any solution. Help us to know the

infinite strength which is there to meet our weakness. Teach us not to be afraid to ask for some of
that strength, in the little things that are dear to us
as well as in the great issues of the world where we
feel helpless.

V   Christ is risen.
R   **He is risen indeed**.
V   Let us bless the Lord.
R   **Thanks be to God**.

So many miracles when he was walking as a man
among his friends and his enemies, but none to
save or help himself. When he intervened in the
course of things it was to heal or to bring relief
from hunger or fear. Now that his work in the natural body was finished, offered at the end upon
the Cross, the last and greatest miracle of the
Father's power threw open his tomb, to set free
into the world eternal life for all who would
accept the grace of his triumph over death.

You foolish men, his enemies – you thought
that an official seal and an armed guard could put
an end to your troubles. You feared him when he
gathered the crowds around him, and sent your
own crowd to call for his death. You trusted
human law and human judgement, setting the
power of Caesar against the will of God. God

could have destroyed the world in a moment, putting an end to sin and rebellion, and all that had grieved him since the first human disobedience. What can we say to the love that not only spared us, but submitted the fullness of divinity to constraint and suffering and death?

We call for more signs, we will not believe without the reassurance of our senses. I need my own little personal earthquake to remind me that all this is true. I am not just remembering an episode in history, once new and present now only as a page in a book. I am praising the falling of a dark wall that marked the end of life, the opening of a barred gate between living once and living eternally.

✠

Dear Risen Lord, please roll away the stone from my heart.

2

Empty Tomb

V   We adore thee O Christ and we bless thee.
R   **Because by thy glorious Resurrection thou hast given life to the world.**

They found the stone rolled away from the tomb, but when they went in, they did not find the body. (Luke 24:2–3)

His friends had sorrowfully laid in the tomb a body broken with suffering and certified as dead. Now the morning brought a new realization that this had not been the end. The stone that had closed upon their hope had opened upon a hope greater than they had ever known.

We give thanks for the unexpected joys of life; for the solution of problems that had seemed insoluble; for the disappearance of fears and anxieties; for the renewal of hope that has been lost in despair; for the opening of new ways in God's purpose for us.

We give up too easily; we fear that every setback is a disaster; we are anxious for a future that we think we can foresee and understand. Help us to trust from day to day and to find the way to new endeavour in each apparent failure.

V   Christ is risen.
R   **He is risen indeed.**
V   Let us bless the Lord.
R   **Thanks be to God.**

That morning, everyone was thinking about a corpse. Some were thinking good riddance, some mourning for a cruel, incurable loss. There was nowhere else for friends to go, only to look again, with eyes worn by weeping, at the place of sorrow. But the end was the beginning.

That emptiness, the sight of nothing where there should have been something, was a new sight of reality. People were puzzled then and the mystery has never gone away. How can we comprehend and explain mere emptiness, when it is an emptiness full of hope? When the power of life is so giving and yet so demanding, it is more comfortable to think about ways in which a dead body may be lost. But the comfort that God gives is not the cosiness of the familiar.

Can an empty place, a vacant hollow, be the

source of new hope? Graves are places of despair, corruption, superstitious fears. There was no witness of the moment when death was overcome and turned to life, when a dead body became a risen body. It was not Lazarus, a widow's son, a little girl waking up to go on living again. No human eyes could look upon the strangest, holiest place in all the world in its wonder – only in its emptiness.

The Cross for ever stands to mark the great price of our redemption: the Tomb for ever lies open to declare our entry into eternal life.

✠

Risen Lord, keep me and all who believe from living with the dead, the vanished years, the dry bones of time.

Risen Lord, clear out from my soul all that would decay and turn to corruption, darkening the light within.

Risen Lord, whenever it seems that nothing is left, show me that there is so much still to come.

3

Vision of Angels

V   We adore thee O Christ and we bless thee.

R   **Because by thy glorious Resurrection thou hast given life to the world.**

The angel said to the women, 'Do not be afraid: I know that you are looking for Jesus who was crucified. He is not here; for he has been raised, as he said.' (Matt. 28:5–6)

As they stood, frightened and bewildered at the entrance to the tomb, they were given words of guidance and comfort. God had sent his messengers to declare his purpose and make them ready for the revelations that were still to come.

We give thanks for the unseen powers of goodness which surround us and keep us in safety; for all the ways in which God's word comes to us; for continual leading into the right way, even when we do not know that we are being led.

We are always more ready to speak than to listen; more ready to be concerned with our doubts and fears than to rest in quiet confidence. Help us always to be open to the message that may come in strange and unexpected ways and draw us nearer to the Risen Christ.

V   Christ is risen.
R   **He is risen indeed.**
V   Let us bless the Lord.
R   **Thanks be to God.**

Angels of God, his messengers and the guardians of his children, you were given many tasks when Jesus walked on this earth. You announced his coming and praised the glory of his birth. You were with him whenever the human flesh that he had taken became hard to bear, strengthening him in the last agony. You proclaimed his rising from the tomb when the purpose first made known in Galilee was completed in Jerusalem.

Why should God care so much for this little world when he has all the universe at his command and creatures more exalted to do his bidding? Why so much trouble, such divine sorrow, for people who stumble about in error and confusion?

It is easy to imagine an angel as winged and

shining, sharing our human form but infinitely more glorious. Through the centuries of our faith many have made their imagination live in painting and statuary. Few indeed have seen these wonderful creatures, but perhaps we can learn to see the divine messengers working in our own kind. And they may not be in golden armour, but in very humble, obscure lives that are touched by his grace.

Since God took our nature, the gate of life is opened and the human form is made glorious. Angels and humanity are joined in a wonderful order, working together in his service.

✠

Angel of the Annunciation, strengthen my faith.

Angels of the Nativity, open my eyes to the glory of God.

Angel of the Agony, bear me up in the hour of death.

Angels of the Resurrection, lead me to eternal life.

4

Disciples at the Tomb

V   We adore thee O Christ and we bless thee.

R   **Because by thy glorious Resurrection thou hast given life to the world.**

The two disciples were running together, but the other disciple outran Peter and reached the tomb first. He bent down to look in and saw the linen wrappings lying there, but he did not go in. Then Simon Peter came, following him, and went into the tomb. (John 20:4–6)

The disciples kept their distinctive characters, even in this hour of fear and wonder: Peter always rushing into action, the Beloved Disciple more hesitant and full of reverent awe. Different in temperament, they were both called to be witnesses to the truth, then and thereafter.

We give thanks for the diversity of Christian people; for the many gifts used in God's service; for the friendship of other Christians with whom we seek and find the Lord. In the fellowship of the Church,

there is need for many types, drawn together in faith.

We each have our own particular failings, perhaps of impetuosity or timidity, or some other part of our nature which makes our service imperfect. Help us to find the strength that lies hidden in our weakness, so that we may learn in what way we are being called to our Christian duty.

V   Christ is risen.
R   **He is risen indeed.**
V   Let us bless the Lord.
R   **Thanks be to God.**

Running so fast, but still hesitant, loving so much that love dared not venture closer. Was it you, John, the son of Zebedee? You were not so gentle when Jesus called you and your brother Sons of Thunder. You had to bend low to look into that miracle of emptiness, as once wise men had stooped into a stable. Or were you another John, the faithful, well-loved follower, the silent watcher at the Cross? Whoever you were, the love of Jesus opened your eyes to see his glory and to make it known to all the ages.

Of course, Peter went straight in, because it was the next thing to do and no time for thinking. Wait, Peter, your time will come and there will be a special message for you.

It would be so easy to be confused in the amazement of that early morning, to mistake the tomb. But here were the cloths, and you saw them, the last gift of sorrowing friends, the last link with the human body that needed the things of this world. It was no illusion: this was the place where they had laid him.

You had been companions for so long, twelve chosen friends waiting for the coming of the Kingdom. Only yesterday it had seemed that the promise was broken, the company dispersed. It was just beginning, a new and still more glorious fellowship that would hold all time, all people, in God's eternal life.

It holds even me, as surely as it holds those who ran to seek him in the garden on that distant morning.

✝

Risen Lord, make my feet swift to come to you.
Teach me to bend low, from the height of self to humble sharing in the fellowship of the faithful.

5

Mary Magdalene

V   We adore thee O Christ and we bless thee.
R   **Because by thy glorious Resurrection thou hast given life to the world.**

Jesus said to her, 'Mary!' She turned and said to him in Hebrew, 'Rabbouni!' (which means Teacher). Mary Magdalene went and announced to the disciples, 'I have seen the Lord.' (John 20:16, 18)

Mary Magdalene felt so lonely and helpless; she had loved greatly but now her love seemed unable to reach the beloved one. Suddenly it was all changed, and she became the first witness to the salvation of the world.

We give thanks for the gift of discernment; for recognition of Jesus Christ, present in many ways and many places; for the privilege of adoration. We give thanks for all healing of body and mind, for the living power dispelling the dark things that trouble us.

Sometimes we fail to discern the Lord; we think that he has left us, or we do not acknowledge his presence with awe and devotion. Help us to remember that we are never separated from his risen presence and that he is to be worshipped as God of all creation.

V   Christ is risen.
R   **He is risen indeed.**
V   Let us bless the Lord.
R   **Thanks be to God.**

Mary of Magdala, you knew the deep darkness, the horror that is most horrible because it is there inside and has no form to fight. What strange roads did you tread before Jesus, the beloved, came to lead you into the right way? What were the seven devils who had you in their power before he drove them away to their own place?

We try to explain you, Mary, who had so much to give in love returned for love. We use our words to cover our own disquiet, and talk of psychosis, delusion, lack of self-esteem. We make light of devils, the dreadful things of evil that Jesus knew and conquered. He knew that the power of darkness was no foolish imagination.

It seemed too cruel, the dawn that brought no relief. The devils were coming back, and there was no one to keep them out. Even the loved body, broken and cold in death, had been taken away. You wanted to find him, to treat him tenderly even though he could not feel your love.

But you were the first one, Mary of Magdala, the first to see beyond the puzzling emptiness to the new presence, the Lord more powerful, more beautiful than even you had seen him before. No wonder you wanted to cling to him, to hold him for ever so that the darkness would never come again. But there was work for you, a message for one woman to bring life back to those foolish, frightened men. The greatest, strangest words that human lips could ever speak were yours that day: 'I have seen the Lord.'

✠

Teacher, Master, Lord, when the devils start to come close and shut out the light of my day, give me your strength to defend my weakness. Call me by my name, and make me turn to you.

6

Simon Peter

V We adore thee O Christ and we bless thee.
R **Because by thy glorious Resurrection thou hast given life to the world.**

The Lord has risen indeed, and he has appeared to Simon. (Luke 24:34)
He appeared to Cephas. (1 Cor. 15:5)

Peter must have been distracted with shame and sorrow all through the long hours after the crucifixion. He had denied his Master and betrayed the trust which he had sworn to keep even if he had to die with Jesus. Then, in a moment of wonder, he knew that all was forgiven and that he would be entrusted with even greater things than before.

We give thanks for the gift of repentance; for conviction of sin and assurance of pardon; for all new opportunities, all fresh starts, in each one of which we experience the Resurrection joy.

We are often unwilling to acknowledge our sins; we make excuses; we worry more about what peo-

ple think of us than of the offence against God. Help us to grasp and hold fast the absolute love that pardons all offences, asking only for true sorrow and a resolve to do better.

V   Christ is risen.
R   **He is risen indeed**.
V   Let us bless the Lord.
R   **Thanks be to God.**

Dear Simon Peter, you were not very like a rock: you always opened your mouth without thinking, and often got it wrong.

'Let's put up tents and stay on this mountain.'

'You mustn't go up to Jerusalem to suffer.'

'Don't wash my feet – wash me all over.'

'All the rest may run away, but I never will.'

Even after that panic flight in the garden, you had courage to follow into the place of trial, but then in fear three times denied your Master.

The Resurrection morning found you still impetuous, the first to rush into the empty tomb.

And so it went on, jumping into the sea to be the first to greet the Lord on shore, coming at last to know that the good news was not only for the Jewish people but for all the world.

Dear Peter, I understand so well the foolish speaking, wished the next moment unsaid; the hurtful sayings that will not go away; the embarrassment that worms its way into the place of repentance, making wounded self-esteem feel like sorrow for sin.

How unbelievable it was when Mary Magdalene was told, 'Go and tell his disciples and Peter.'

And Peter? Peter the coward, the one who denied him? Yes, a special message of love for Peter.

The last time you saw him in the old life, he looked on you with such sorrowful eyes that there was nothing left but bitter tears and despair.

Many times I dare not look into the eyes of Jesus, but he compels me, draws me into the assurance of being forgiven, of sharing in the life that is for ever new.

✠

Father, look on that beloved face and find my likeness there.

Peter usually got it wrong, but once, in a moment of ultimate truth, he knew that Jesus was the Christ, the Son of the living God.

May I know the presence of God in the Risen Christ who calls me.

7

Closed Room

V We adore thee O Christ and we bless thee.
R **Because by thy glorious Resurrection thou hast given light to the world.**

When it was evening on that day, the first day of the week, and the doors of the house where the disciples had met were locked for fear of the Jews, Jesus came and stood among them and said, 'Peace be with you.' (John 20:19)

The disciples were still full of anxiety; the new hope that Jesus had risen did not overcome their fear of their human enemies. As they met in secret, their Lord came to them with the word of peace: no doors or locks could keep him out.

We give thanks for the peace that comes through Jesus Christ; we rejoice in his presence in our lives; in prayer, in sacraments, in every moment; even when we are anxious and preoccupied with the cares of this world.

We close our hearts against the love of God, as the disciples closed their doors; we allow ourselves to be imprisoned by our fears and doubts. Help us to be open always to the coming of Christ, to receive the assurance of his peace and to proclaim him with confidence.

V   Christ is risen.
R   **He is risen indeed.**
V   Let us bless the Lord.
R   **Thanks be to God.**

So short a time since that last meal together, perhaps in the very room. Three days ago, they were all together, the fellowship unbroken, promising fidelity even to death. Then a night and a day of terror, a day of sorrow, a day of rumours and visions – they were weary, bewildered, unable to take any more.

Close the doors against the world that threatens and destroys.

Close the doors against the people who come to us, for they may bring trouble.

Close the doors against the Lord who knocks and will not leave us alone.

Surely he comes in anger, in accusation of sin, comes to avenge the broken promises, the betrayal, the desertion. He is the God of justice, visiting iniquity.

But no, he comes in peace, in love, the God of mercy and pardon. Wounded, he comes to heal all wounds. The grave could not keep him in, the doors cannot keep him out. He is not outside, he is here, he is among us as in the days that have gone, he is everywhere.

The day broke without hope, dark and menacing; now in the evening there is light and joy. Lord, what can we say, what can we do but receive with grace your word of peace.

It was the first day of the week, the first day of the new creation. The old power of sin and death had been broken and the power of life was filling the world, to restore the fellowship and make all things new.

✠

Risen Lord, make me hear your voice and open my closed heart.

Come to me in the morning and in the evening.

8

Thomas

V   We adore thee O Christ and we bless thee.
R   **Because by thy glorious Resurrection thou hast given life to the world.**

Jesus said to him, 'Have you believed because you have seen me? Blessed are those who have not seen and yet have come to believe.' (John 20:29)

Thomas was always the pessimist: not so much a sceptic or doubter as a man who could not believe that the future held anything good. He would not accept the word of the other disciples, but insisted on personally seeing and touching the Risen Lord; but when he saw, his faith was great and he said, 'My Lord and my God!'

We give thanks for all the signs of Christ's Resurrection: for the words of Scripture, for the faith of the Church through the ages, for every realization of Christ in our own lives. We give thanks that we have the promise of blessing on our faith: we do not judge by sight, but trust to see the Lord in his glory.

We are slow to believe; we demand evidence to answer any questions that we choose to ask. Help us to know that Jesus Christ is Lord and God, and to hold fast to him in faith.

V   Christ is risen.
R   **He is risen indeed.**
V   Let us bless the Lord.
R   **Thanks be to God.**

No, Thomas, you never believed that all would be well. You were no coward, you loved Jesus in a dogged, despairing way, ready as you thought to go and die with him at Bethany when Lazarus was raised. On that last night together, you wanted to know exactly where he was going, to be shown the way without any question.

Why did you have to be the one who was absent when he came in his new life to the others – you of all who would not hope for this last and greatest miracle? Was it the purpose that you should go through another week, seven whole days of doubt and sorrow to test your faith and bring the more splendid affirmation?

Ten of them were content to see and believe, but you demanded more, to touch and feel the dreadful wounds. You got your wish, because God may take us at our word and give us more than we expected, more than we really desired. Those marks of suffering showed that this was no ghost, no clever resuscitation – this was something beyond experience or dreams.

You had your part to play, a great part. You made the confession of divinity that silences all argument, bringing a blessing on every generation of believers, though they too might be often anxious and uncertain.

✠

What is my part, insecure and doubting as I too often am?

Lord, you were very patient with Thomas, and made him at last a man of hope and trust.

Be patient with me, when I doubt and hesitate because the good news seems too good to be true.
   Lord, I believe: help my unbelief.

9

Emmaus

V We adore thee O Christ and we bless thee.
R **Because by thy glorious Resurrection thou hast given life to the world.**

When he was at the table with them, he took bread, blessed and broke it, and gave it to them. Then their eyes were opened, and they recognized him. (Luke 24:30–31)

Two of the disciples walked and talked with Jesus for a time without knowing who he was. It was only when they sat down to a meal that the familiar actions recalled their table fellowship with him and they knew that he was present with them again.

We give thanks for the Holy Communion in which we are united with Jesus Christ in the broken bread and the poured wine. We praise God for this wonderful sacrament, in which we receive his grace and strength to draw near in love.

We too often neglect the opportunity for Communion; we find excuses for staying away; we come without proper preparation; our devotion is cold and distracted. Help us to reverence the mystery of the Body and Blood of Christ, so that we can continually meet him and know him in the breaking of bread.

V   Christ is risen.
R   **He is risen indeed.**
V   Let us bless the Lord.
R   **Thanks be to God.**

It was a long road, so late in the day, still hot and dusty though the shadows were lengthening. Two of you went on together, walking away from the city of sorrow, the city of rumours and of hopes too daring to be believed. Three days of loss had left you weary, no longer open to trust what others had seen.

A stranger can be menacing or friendly. This one wanted to know what you were talking about and you welcomed him into your trouble and found comfort in his words, old truths seen in a new light. Then, hospitality stronger than weariness, you took him into your home. He might have gone on, but you invited him to stay.

Then it all came back to you – the meals together, his wonderful words that chastened and encouraged, the peace of his presence. He was still yours, your teacher, your friend. The beloved body was back there before your eyes, but with new power to come and go, to be everywhere. He would always be close to you, even when you did not see him, as he had drawn close to you on the road.

How you rushed back, the meal unfinished, no longer tired but eager with the good news. As you ran to tell of him, you were running to see him again, in the city that was no longer sorrowful.

✠

Risen Lord, open my eyes to recognize you, in whatever way you will reveal yourself.

Risen Lord, open the Scriptures to me, because they all speak to me of you.

Risen Lord, come to me in the stranger, in the guest, in the bread and wine of your own banquet.

FACIAM VOS FIERI PISCAT RES HMNVM

E·LIBRIS·DESMOND·CHVTE

10

Galilee

V   We adore thee O Christ and we bless thee.
R   **Because by thy glorious Resurrection thou hast given life to the world.**

Just after daybreak, Jesus stood on the beach; but the disciples did not know that it was Jesus . . . When they had gone ashore, they saw a charcoal fire there, with fish on it, and bread. (John 21:4, 9)

The disciples returned to Galilee and went back to their former work. The Lord whom they had seen in Jerusalem was there before them, as he had promised. God and Lord of all, he still came to them as one who served, and prepared a meal for them.

We give thanks for food; for the simple necessities and pleasures of life. We praise God for sustaining us and supplying all our needs. We praise him because he holds all things in his power and yet cares for each, keeping us in life now and leading us towards everlasting life.

We are not thankful enough for our food and for the other blessings of our lives; we do not always remember to give thanks before we eat; we do not think enough about those who are in want. Help us always to have grateful hearts and to be mindful of the needs of others.

V   Christ is risen.
R   **He is risen indeed.**
V   Let us bless the Lord.
R   **Thanks be to God.**

Some of you went back to the familiar lake, back to the places that spoke of home and a life that did not look beyond the routine of every day. Back to where things might go on as they had been before Jesus came to break and make you. But the world had changed, newly created in a new covenant that demanded less and yet infinitely more.

Tokens of the past were returning, but nothing ever happens twice in the same way. It was another dawn, and you would never see the sunrise without remembering the garden, the empty tomb on the first day of eternal life.

There was a great catch after a barren night, just as when he came and preached from the boat, and then called you to follow; but this time, the net was not broken. Peter, of course you were first on shore, wild to meet the Lord you had once begged to leave you in your sinfulness. There was a new challenge for you that morning, love questioning love so that it might be strengthened.

There was bread and fish, the simple things once wonderfully multiplied in the wilderness to meet a crisis of success. Another meal together, as there had been so many in the past, until that last one on the evening of sorrow. This was a beginning, a new feeding of more than the hungry bodies. For your Lord had work for you: his teaching, his empowering you had thought was lost was more wonderful, irresistible, turning sheep into shepherds.

✠

Risen Lord, let me feel your presence every morning.

Go on teaching me to discern the tokens of Resurrection in my life and in other lives and in the world around me.

Feed me so that I may feed your sheep.

11

Five Hundred Witnesses

V   We adore thee O Christ and we bless thee.
R   **Because by thy glorious Resurrection thou hast given life to the world.**

Then he appeared to more than five hundred brothers and sisters at one time, most of whom are still alive, though some have died. (1 Cor. 15:6)

This appearance may have taken place in Galilee, where many of the people had believed in Jesus, though some think it is a reference to the Pentecost experience. Whether in Galilee or Jerusalem, the number of witnesses to the Resurrection was dramatically increased.

We give thanks for the millions of our fellow Christians with whom we are one in the Lord; for the friendship of those who are close to us in our own family of faith; for all the witnesses who have gone before us to share in the Resurrection.

We sometimes become self-centred in our faith and forget that we are part of a great company that

no one can number, in which each is equally precious in the sight of God. Help us to live as members of the Body of Christ, always more eager for the good of others than for our own.

V   Christ is risen.
R   **He is risen indeed**.
V   Let us bless the Lord.
R   **Thanks be to God**.

Who were you, the nameless, the unrecorded, not set down in Scripture or remembered in the festivals of saints? Had you gathered for worship when your Lord appeared to you, or did he break into a working day, bringing some little town to a halt in shared adoration?

You were not called to go out into the world, to the despised Samaritans, the unknown Gentiles, to confront the power of Rome by sea and land to its farthest limits. You had to go on living, witnesses in the workshop, by the lake, or in the family dwelling. You were to be the first of the faithful who did no great deeds, who are not enrolled among the saints and scholars, the missionaries and martyrs. You are our ancestors in the faith.

He comes to us still, unheralded, unexpected, when we are recollected in worship or distracted by the demands of the hour. He is the quiet presence that says, 'Go on, be faithful, take the next few steps in the narrow path before you.' Or he may be the sudden illumination that changes everything, lighting a road that we did not know was there.

What they shared that day, five hundred together, was not forgotten in harder times. The threat of hostile power, the sorrows of life in a fallen world, the weary annoyances of day after day: these did not break the fellowship of having seen God and lived, to have grasped eternity, though some had died.

✠

Risen Lord, keep me in loving fellowship with all who share the faith, who have known your presence. Unite me with the great company who have kept the vision to the end and are gathered into fullness of life.

Whenever and wherever you come to me, make me ready to receive you.

12

James

V We adore thee O Christ and we bless thee.
R **Because by thy glorious Resurrection thou hast given life to the world.**

Then he appeared to James. (1 Cor. 15:7)

The human family of Jesus did not at first understand who he was; indeed, some of them thought that he was mad. James, called the brother of the Lord, was changed by his experience of the Risen Christ into a devout believer and a leader of the Church in Jerusalem.

We give thanks for our families; for the home which is a small but wonderful image of the divine care; for the nurture of human love and understanding; for all those with whom we share our lives.

We do not always value those who are closest to us; we become impatient and familiarity makes us careless in our consideration of others. Help us to care for those who have been given us as our

families here on earth and to make our homes centres of love and happiness.

V   Christ is risen.
R   **He is risen indeed.**
V   Let us bless the Lord.
R   **Thanks be to God.**

It was such a late coming to you who had been so close in life, even though you had not been his companion in the times of showing and the times of trouble. Not for you the sudden glory of the first morning, certainty that a new world had begun. What did you think, as the days passed and there was no sign? When you heard them speak of the wonder they had seen, did you still not believe? Did you think it was illusion, or did you grow resentful that he had not shown himself to you?

The privilege granted to five hundred must have seemed too much to bear. Perhaps you felt guilty that you had rejected him, tried to turn him from his chosen way, called him mad. Or did you still think you had been right, the others wrong who had followed him and now said that he was alive again? Not one of his chosen Twelve, could you hope to share in his new commission?

Then it came, the revelation that dispelled all doubt, cancelled resentment, washed out the stain of guilt. You, who thought you had been rejected from following, were called to lead. In the years ahead you would have to make decisions for his infant Church.

✠

Risen Lord, guide me to recognize you in the close and familiar things.

Let me know you in the dull routine of every day, so that I may be always ready for the moments when your presence is strong and clear.

Teach me to trust the words of all who have witnessed to you from the beginning of the Church until now.

And please, care for those who are dear to me, and keep them firm in faith and hope and love.

13

Ascension

V   We adore thee O Christ and we bless thee.

R   **Because by thy glorious Resurrection thou hast given life to the world.**

While he was blessing them, he withdrew from them and was carried up to heaven. And they worshipped him, and returned to Jerusalem with great joy. (Luke 24:51–2)

The first parting from Jesus on Calvary had been sorrow and shame for the disciples. When he went from them a second time they were full of hope and joy because they knew that he was alive for ever and that they would see him again.

We give thanks for the Ascension of Jesus Christ, in which our human nature is lifted up into the mystery of divinity. We know that we shall follow where he has gone before and we praise God for the restoration of the human race to the holiness that was lost by sin.

We misuse the life that we have been given, forgetting that it comes from God and will return to him; we are held too closely by the cares and desires of this world. Help us to know where true joy is to be found and to direct our lives towards Christ in his glory.

V   Christ is risen.
R   **He is risen indeed.**
V   Let us bless the Lord.
R   **Thanks be to God.**

Some of you had seen him transfigured on the hill of glory; all had shared the horror of the hill of death. Now you stood upon the hill of promise and watched him go.

That was a heavy command to lay on you Galileans: witnessing to the Judaeans who despised you as uncouth provincials, to the Samaritans you despised as heretics, to the whole unknown world of Gentiles beyond the seas and beyond the Law. Because he had taught you that all were the children of God, you went back into the city not trembling with fear but full of joy.

In all the times of seeing your Master after the day of his rising, the joy had been mingled with awe and often with his words of correction. Now, at the last encounter, there was only confidence, a strength that no human power could give or take away.

You could have stood there watching, as Peter had wanted to stay on the hill of glory. Eyes that had seen such wonder must look to the world below, feet that had followed him must take the path down into the busy day. There was work to be done, a break in the fellowship to mend, a church to be built.

It would all be enabled through prayer not to a God remote, unimaginable, dangerous to look upon, but to one who had shown his human face, one they had loved as a friend. He had left his last bequest to them – a world made holy because divine steps had graced it on human feet.

✠

Ascended Lord, lift up my heart above all doubts and fears.

Ascended Lord, lift up my eyes to see what you have for me to do.

Ascended Lord, lift up my voice to be your witness, because these frail human things are for ever made holy.

14

Paul

V   We adore thee O Christ and we bless thee.
R   **Because by thy glorious Resurrection thou hast
given life to the world.**

*Last of all, as to someone untimely born, he
appeared also to me. For I am the least of the apostles, unfit to be called an apostle, because I persecuted the church of God. But by the grace of God I
am what I am, and his grace towards me has not
been in vain.* (1 Cor. 15:8–10)

Paul was a ruthless persecutor of Christians until
the Risen Christ appeared to him. The encounter
with the Lord changed him into a great teacher of
the faith, called to spread the word of salvation
into the Gentile world.

**We give thanks for the gift of faith that comes from
God and not from our seeking; for the love that
changes us; for the grace that makes us able to do
what we could never do in our own strength.**

We will not always listen when God is calling us; we go on our own ways of pride and self-will. Help us to remember in whom we have believed and to live more worthily of such a great salvation.

V   Christ is risen.
R   **He is risen indeed.**
V   Let us bless the Lord.
R   **Thanks be to God.**

He came so late to you, making you born again at a time when change seemed impossible, out of place. At the time of your deepest hostility, anger and malice towards him, he came to you, and the light dawned.

Light is God's first gift, but light can be unbearable, rending the sight that it comes to illumine. It takes time to adjust to God's new light, to turn around and open the eyes to look in another direction, to change Saul to Paul, a new name, a new heart.

When you fell down on the road, did you have a vision of what was to come, the suffering, the sorrow of new believers fallen away?

Did you ever see him when he walked among the people? Did you pass him by without a thought, or were you one of those who murmured against him, feared him and planned his death?

Now you had to meet those who knew and loved him as their Master. You had to make friends of enemies, those you would have killed, who still mourned the killing of Stephen.

The great command came to you as it had come to them, to go out into all the world and tell the good news. Your life was given to the one you had persecuted, the one the others had denied and deserted. You joined with them in love, because all shared the failures and the grace.

You more than any knew the reality of sin forgiven, perfect love calling for the love that suffers long and is kind.

✠

Risen Lord, come to me early and late, for all time is yours.

Risen Lord, give me your perfect light, and the strength to receive it.

Risen Lord, let me walk with you, to the edge of my little world.

After the Stations

Almighty God, whose only-begotten Son died on the Cross for our salvation and was raised from the dead to restore us to eternal life, mercifully grant that as we have followed the way of his Resurrection we may through grace be dead to sin and alive to his continual presence with us; through the same Jesus Christ our Lord. Amen.

A hymn may be sung; the following are suitable:

'Jesus lives!'

'Rejoice, the Lord is King'

'The strife is o'er'

'Thine be the glory'

A priest who is present may give this blessing; or the people may say it together, saying, 'us' for 'you':

Now the God of peace, that brought again from the dead our Lord Jesus, that great shepherd of the sheep, through the blood of the everlasting covenant, make you *perfect in every good work to do his will, working in* you *that which is well pleasing in his sight: and the blessing of God Almighty, the Father, the Son and the Holy Spirit, be among* you *and remain with* you *always. Amen.*

A Note on the Illustrations
by Winefride Pruden

page i: Christ crowned
© *Eric Gill for* The Four Gospels of Our Lord Jesus Christ, *published by Robert Gibbings at the Golden Cockerel Press, 1931.*

This wood-engraving is almost too rich in symbolism: 'death is swallowed up in victory' and the cross has become the tree of life. The stylized foliage, reminiscent of Romanesque art, is typical of Gill. The word 'PAX' on the archway not only refers to Christ as the Prince of Peace, but also declares Gill's own pacifism. The figures in the background remind us that in the early 1930s Gill was also working on his carved panels for Broadcasting House, in London, which included reliefs of the Sower and Ariel playing a pipe. A further personal note, since Gill was a Dominican tertiary, is the Hound of St Dominic.

Before the Stations
See under James *overleaf.*

1 Earthquake
© *Timothy Holloway, c. 1965.*
'He is risen as he said, Alleluia!'
Timothy Holloway is the son of the painter, etcher and engraver, Edgar Holloway. He grew up in the Ditchling community and made this print when he was about sixteen. He is now a freelance typographical designer.

2 Empty Tomb
© *Eric Gill, 1917.*
This wood-engraving was made originally for *The Game*, an occasional magazine published by St Dominic's Press between 1916 and 1923. It was intended primarily for the friends and well-wishers of Eric Gill and Hilary Pepler and included illustrations by Gill, David Jones, Desmond Chute and the children of Pepler and Gill.

3 Vision of Angels
© *Eric Gill, 1931.*
One of the forty-one wood-engravings made for *The Four Gospels of Our Lord Jesus Christ.* The Evangelists differ slightly in their accounts of the first Easter Sunday morning. Here, Gill seems to have sought a compromise between Matthew's 'angel whose face shone like lightning' and Mark's 'youth wearing a white robe'.

4 Disciples at the Tomb

© *Eric Gill for* The Passion of Our Lord Jesus Christ, *published by Faber and Faber, 1934.*

Gill may have had a particular affection for this book because it was printed by Hague and Gill, the press which he set up with his son-in-law, René Hague. This illustration was chosen for his own memorial card in 1940.

5 Mary Magdalene

© *David Jones for* A Child's Rosary Book, *published by St Dominic's Press, 1924.*

The craft of wood-engraving could not have been farther removed from David Jones's characteristic drawings and paintings with their cobweb line and rainwashed colour. It was a comparatively new departure for him and his lack of facility in the medium forced him to simplify and confine himself to bold, tonal contrasts which, even on a small scale, give an impression of monumentality.

6 Simon Peter

© *Eric Gill, 1931.*

Another of the wood-engravings for *The Four Gospels of Our Lord Jesus Christ*, regarded as a masterpiece of book production, successfully combining text and illustration as this example shows. The type is Gill's Golden Cockerel which was designed exclusively for the Golden Cockerel Press in 1929.

7 Closed Room *and* **After the Stations**
Wood-engraving by © Philip Hagreen, printed by the Ditchling Press (successor to St Dominic's Press) originally for an ordination card, c. 1938.
Jesus reveals himself to all the apostles except Thomas. They recognize his pierced hand in the sign of peace.

8 Thomas *and* **9 Emmaus**
© Eric Gill, 1931.
Two further wood-engravings for Robert Gibbings' *The Four Gospels of Our Lord Jesus Christ.*

10 Galilee
I will make you fishers of men
© David Jones, wood-engraving, 1925.
In this book-plate for Desmond Chute, who taught him wood-engraving, David Jones uses Latin abbreviations current in medieval MSS. He almost certainly learned these from Fr Vincent McNabb OP. Some of his letters appear to be facing the wrong way. He probably did this accidentally the first time (most novice wood-engravers forget that letters have to be reversed) and liked the variety it introduced.

Illustrations 5, 10 and 11 reproduced by courtesy of the David Jones Trustees.

11 Five Hundred Witnesses
© *David Jones, wood-engraving for* A Child's
Rosary Book, *op cit.*
As St Paul does not say when Jesus appeared to the
five hundred witnesses, this choice of illustration
follows the opinion that it may have happened on
the day of Pentecost when, we are told in the Acts
of the Apostles, a great crowd gathered to hear the
apostles speaking in many tongues.

12 James
Wood-engraving by © *Philip Hagreen, published
by the Ditchling Press.*
St Paul tantalizingly does not tell us which St James
was favoured with this personal revelation.
Authorities differ, but the consensus of opinion
seems to support James called 'the brother of the
Lord', of whose subsequent history we read in the
Acts of the Apostles and in Galatians.

13 Ascension
© *Eric Gill, 1918.*
Made for *The Game.* One of Eric Gill's few wood-
cuts, noticeably different in technique from the
wood-engravings with their final detail.

14 Paul

Drawing © David Jones and wood-engraving ©
Eric Gill, 1937.

The more vivid imagination of the draughtsman,
combined with the greater facility of line typical of
the wood-engraver, results in a unique composi-
tion. It represents St Paul in the ship on his way
from Caesarea to prison in Rome. The stigmata
borne by St Paul may be explained as one of the
many theories (an unlikely one) propounded for
'the thorn in the flesh' referred to by St Paul in
2 Corinthians 12:7. It was more likely a recurring
illness.

Winefride Pruden
Ditchling
March 1998